JESSICA SIMPSON
ALL-AMERICAN
FASHION ENTREPRENEUR

Jessica Rusick

Checkerboard Library

An Imprint of Abdo Publishing
abdobooks.com

abdobooks.com

Published by Abdo Publishing, a division of ABDO, PO Box 398166, Minneapolis, Minnesota 55439. Copyright © 2020 by Abdo Consulting Group, Inc. International copyrights reserved in all countries. No part of this book may be reproduced in any form without written permission from the publisher. Checkerboard Library™ is a trademark and logo of Abdo Publishing.

Printed in the United States of America, North Mankato, Minnesota
052019
092019

THIS BOOK CONTAINS RECYCLED MATERIALS

Design: Aruna Rangarajan, Mighty Media, Inc.
Production: Mighty Media, Inc.
Editor: Rebecca Felix
Design Elements: Shutterstock Images
Cover Photograph: AP Images
Interior Photographs: Everett Collection NYC, p. 13; Getty Images, pp. 17, 21, 23, 25; Seth Poppel/Yearbook Library, pp. 7, 9; Shutterstock Images, pp. 5, 11, 15, 19, 27, 28 (left, middle, right), 29 (middle, bottom); theunquietlibrarian/Flickr, p. 29 (top)

Library of Congress Control Number: 2018966466

Publisher's Cataloging-in-Publication Data

Names: Rusick, Jessica, author.
Title: Jessica Simpson: all-American fashion entrepreneur / by Jessica Rusick
Other title: All-American fashion entrepreneur
Description: Minneapolis, Minnesota : Abdo Publishing, 2020 | Series: Fashion figures | Includes online resources and index.
Identifiers: ISBN 9781532119545 (lib. bdg.) | ISBN 9781532174001 (ebook)
Subjects: LCSH: Simpson, Jessica (Jessica Johnson), 1980- --Juvenile literature. | Fashion designers--United States--Biography--Juvenile literature. | Television personalities--Biography--Juvenile literature. | Singers--Biography--Juvenile literature. | Women entrepreneurs--Biography--Juvenile literature.
Classification: DDC 746.920922 [B]--dc23

CONTENTS

Famous Fashionista 4

A Natural Talent 6

Music & TV Star 10

First Film & Fashion Lines 12

A New Direction 16

Body-Positive Designer 18

Executive Decisions & Expanding Family 22

Steady Success 26

Timeline 28

Glossary 30

Online Resources 31

Index 32

FAMOUS FASHIONISTA

Jessica Simpson is a singer, actress, and fashion **entrepreneur**. She has a billion-dollar fashion empire. Her style is trendy yet simple and **accessible**. People came to love Simpson's personality and style when she starred on a reality TV show in 2003. The show's success helped launch Simpson's career as a fashion icon!

In 2005, Simpson **debuted** a shoe line called the Jessica Simpson Collection. She expanded the collection to include clothing, and her brand took off. Today, the Jessica Simpson Collection sells everything from clothes to bedding to luggage in 65 countries worldwide.

Simpson strives to understand what everyday women want to wear. Her brand makes body-positive items. Simpson wants her clothing to make wearers with all types of bodies feel fashionable.

Through her fashion line, Simpson has become known as a successful businesswoman. But her first love was singing. Simpson dreamed of being a famous singer since she was young.

Fashion critics have described Jessica Simpson Collection styles as bold, girly, and All-American.

A NATURAL TALENT

Jessica Ann Simpson was born on July 10, 1980, in Abilene, Texas. She grew up in Richardson, Texas. Jessica's father, Joe, was a youth minister. Her mother, Tina, was a stay-at-home parent. Jessica has one younger sister, Ashlee.

From a young age, Jessica loved to sing in the choir at her father's church. Jessica's parents recognized that their daughter had a gift for singing. By the time she was 11, Jessica wanted to be a famous singer. When she was 12, the Disney Channel announced that it was looking for young singers and actors to star on its popular TV show *The Mickey Mouse Club*. Jessica was eager to try out.

Jessica was one of over 50,000 children who **auditioned** for *The Mickey Mouse Club*. After rounds of auditions, she became one of six finalists! However, Jessica was not picked for the show. She was heartbroken. But Jessica's parents told her not to give up on her singing career. And soon, another opportunity came along.

Jessica (*left*) attended J. J. Pearce High School in Richardson, Texas. She dropped out when her fame rose, later getting a General Education Development diploma.

When Jessica was 13, record **producer** DeForest "Buster" Soaries was a guest speaker at the summer church camp she was attending. During this visit, Soaries heard Jessica singing. He was impressed. Soaries asked Jessica to record a CD with his record company!

Jessica was thrilled. She recorded music for her album over the next three years. However, the record company went **bankrupt** before it could release Jessica's CD to the public. Jessica was heartbroken again. And again, her family stepped in to encourage her. This time, they also helped finance her dream.

Jessica's grandmother paid to make copies of Jessica's CD. Jessica toured churches across the country with her father to sell the CDs. On this tour, she promoted her music through performances. Jessica's father acted as her tour manager and her mother her stylist.

The tour helped Jessica earn singing **auditions**. One was with music company Columbia Records. The head of the company, Tommy Mottola, was impressed by Jessica's voice. He also felt she had a sweet, wholesome appeal.

Mottola was sure Americans would love Jessica. In 1997, his company signed her to their label! Sixteen-year-old Jessica began recording her first pop music album.

Jessica recording music as a junior in high school

MUSIC & TV STAR

Simpson released her first album, *Sweet Kisses*, in 1999. The song "I Wanna Love You Forever" was a hit! Simpson's singing dreams were coming true. But it was on TV that her fame would skyrocket.

Simpson's father, Joe, thought being on a reality TV show could help make Simpson more popular and help her music career. In 2002, Simpson married fellow singer Nick Lachey. He was a member of pop group 98 Degrees. Joe convinced TV network VH1 to make a show about the couple.

Newlyweds: Nick & Jessica **debuted** in 2003. On the show, Simpson came across to some viewers as **ditzy**. The media made fun of her intelligence because she acted silly. But millions of Americans found Simpson's behavior funny and relatable.

Newlyweds helped make Simpson's music more popular. She released her third album, *In This Skin*, the same day the show debuted. It became Simpson's best-selling album!

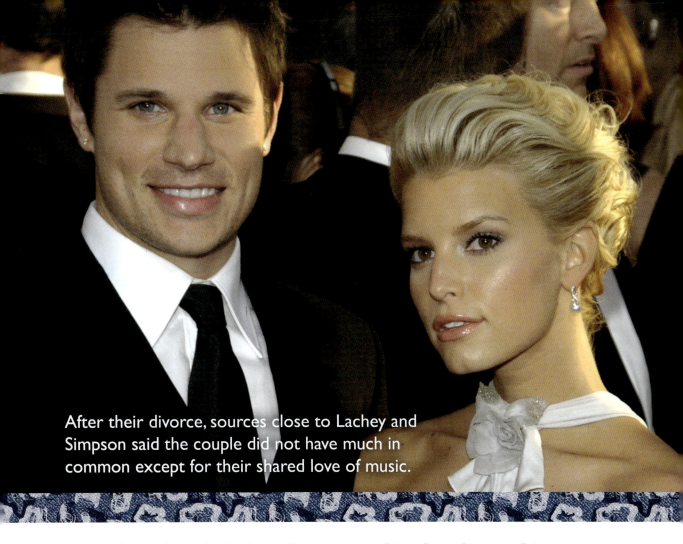

After their divorce, sources close to Lachey and Simpson said the couple did not have much in common except for their shared love of music.

Newlyweds ended when Simpson and Lachey divorced in 2005. But the show had made Simpson more popular than ever, even earning her acting roles. In 2005, she played Daisy Duke in *The Dukes of Hazzard*. Simpson's fashion in this film inspired her future!

FIRST FILM & FASHION LINES

Fashion **entrepreneurs** took notice of Simpson's popularity. They saw that people liked her fashion sense. In 2004, clothing company Tarrant Apparel Group asked Simpson to develop a fashion line. It would **debut** in 2005 to help promote *The Dukes of Hazzard*.

Simpson's fashion line had two labels. JS by Jessica Simpson sold affordably priced tops and low-rise jeans. Princy sold slightly more expensive items. Simpson gave design input on both labels.

Both labels' clothing was meant to be fun and relatable, just like Simpson was to her fans. Items included frilly shirts and jean shorts inspired by Simpson's character Daisy Duke.

Department stores across the country agreed to sell Simpson's clothing. But the line ran into problems after the clothing was made. Tarrant ran out of money and couldn't deliver as much clothing as it had promised buyers. It also did not have enough money for advertising. Without ads, stores could not **market** the clothes.

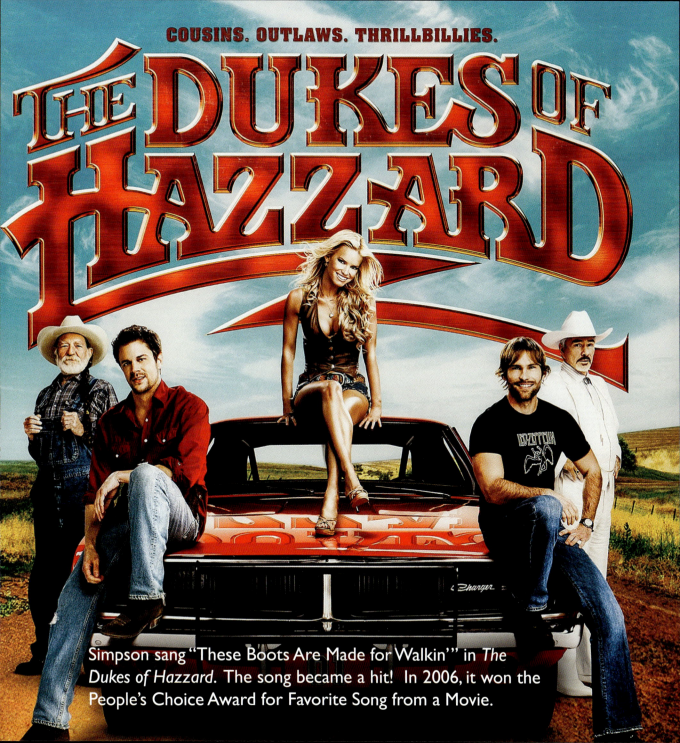

Retail chain Charming Shoppes had agreed to sell Simpson's clothing. But the chain became upset with Tarrant and canceled its order. Tarrant **executives** blamed Simpson for the failure. They said she did not put enough effort into **marketing**. The executives said this was the reason Charming Shoppes canceled its order.

Tarrant was also upset by Simpson's response to a fashion writer who asked about her favorite denim brand. The company thought Simpson should have named her own brand, but she did not.

In 2006, Tarrant sued Simpson for not promoting her brands. Simpson sued Tarrant back, saying it had failed to raise the money it had promised. In 2007, Tarrant ended its relationship with Simpson and shut down the brands.

But Simpson's time in fashion was not over. During her fallout with Tarrant, she had partnered with shoe **entrepreneur** Vince Camuto. Camuto saw **potential** in Simpson. He wanted to help her become a fashion icon.

FASHION FACT

In 2004, Simpson released a line of dessert-themed beauty products called Dessert Beauty. The line was shut down in 2006.

In December 2005, Simpson won VH1's Big in '05 Big Stylin' award. The cable television award honored the year's top style icon in pop culture.

A NEW DIRECTION

Camuto had wanted to work with Simpson for many years. He had seen her reality show in 2003 and was charmed by her personality. Ever since then, he had waited for the opportunity to develop a brand with Simpson. Camuto reached out to Simpson in 2005 after her relationship with Tarrant became strained.

That year, Camuto worked with Simpson on a shoe line called the Jessica Simpson Collection. Camuto had spent **decades** developing high-heeled women's shoes and knew footwear well. His designs used foam and rubber to make even the tallest shoes feel comfortable.

Simpson was founder and **CEO** of the Jessica Simpson Collection. Shoes in the line took style cues from her personal tastes and life. The line's first shoe was a cowboy boot inspired by her movie character Daisy Duke.

Simpson's line became known for its comfortable, fashionable shoes. It earned $50 million in 2005. In 2006, Camuto and Simpson

Simpson (*third from left*) and Vince Camuto pose with models wearing clothing from Simpson's Princy line in 2005.

expanded the line to include clothing. Camuto was confident in their brand. He **predicted** it would one day be worth $1 billion.

BODY-POSITIVE DESIGNER

Like her shoe line, Simpson's new clothing line was inspired by her personal life. Because Simpson was a public figure, the media often discussed her body and weight. Simpson tried not to take the criticism seriously. She turned to her family and friends for support. She also used the **negative** comments to inspire her fashion line.

Simpson knew the fashion industry could make women feel bad for not fitting into certain styles. She wanted her clothing to show that fashion is for everyone. Her line would be **inclusive** for women of all different body types.

In 2010, Simpson's struggles with body image also inspired her to explore beauty standards around the world. She filmed a **documentary** TV show called *The Price of Beauty*. On the show, Simpson traveled to several countries to learn about their beauty practices.

IN HER OWN WORDS

"No one else can define beauty but me.... I don't care what people have to say about my weight. I think I look great."
—Jessica Simpson

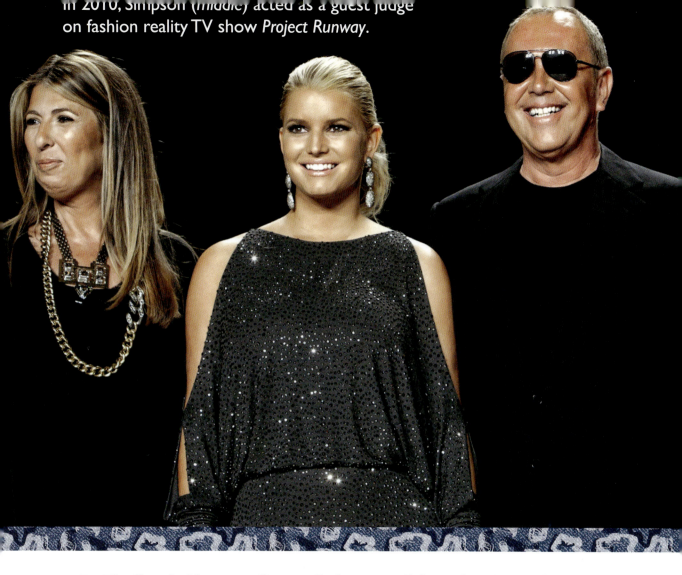

In 2010, Simpson (*middle*) acted as a guest judge on fashion reality TV show *Project Runway*.

In Thailand, Simpson learned about neck lengthening. This is the practice of making someone's neck longer with stiff metal rings.

Beauty **rituals** like this seemed strange to Simpson. But she realized that common American beauty practices, such as wearing high heels, might also seem strange to outsiders.

The Price of Beauty showed that there is no one way to be beautiful. Rather, beauty varies from person to person.

Many women appreciated Simpson's thoughtful approach to beauty. They found comfort in her brand's body positivity. People began to see Simpson as a name in fashion they could trust. Her focus on being **inclusive** helped her growing brand become a fashion empire.

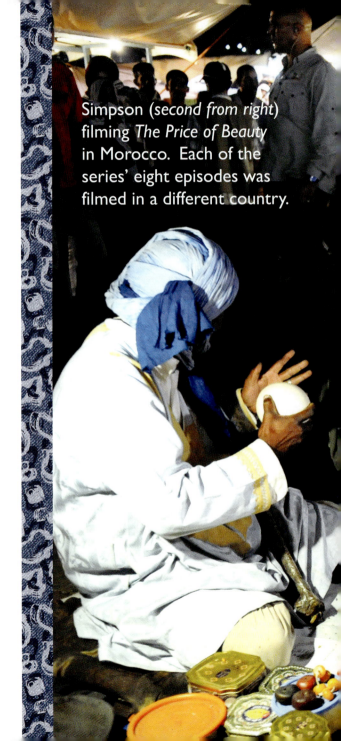

Simpson (*second from right*) filming *The Price of Beauty* in Morocco. Each of the series' eight episodes was filmed in a different country.

EXECUTIVE DECISIONS & EXPANDING FAMILY

Simpson's focus on **inclusive** fashion went beyond body positivity. She felt many fashion brands cared only about wealthy customers in fashion hubs like New York City. But Simpson's Texas roots led her to embrace the fashion needs of women all over the country.

Fashion trends often start in large, urban areas and take time to spread. Simpson believed it was better to see which trends showed staying power before including them in her line. She didn't want her designs to feel foreign to any customers. Waiting for a trend to last meant more customers would be familiar with it and feel comfortable buying her clothes.

Simpson and Camuto employed designers to plan and create new items. But every item in the line received Simpson's approval.

> **IN HER OWN WORDS**
> "People are shocked that they like my brand. Maybe 'cause it's not that expensive? Or maybe because I was a cheesy pop star back in the day? I have no idea."
> —Simpson

Denim clothing and leather accessories were Jessica Simpson Collection staples.

The Jessica Simpson Collection saw continued success. In 2010, it made $750 million. By 2012, the brand expanded into 23 categories. These included sunglasses, jewelry, and handbags.

Simpson's family expanded the same year. In May, Simpson had a daughter, Maxwell, with boyfriend Eric Johnson. The couple had been dating since 2010. Simpson's line released maternity clothes during her pregnancy. In 2013, Simpson and Johnson had a son, Ace. Simpson married Johnson the following year.

In 2014, Simpson's brand reached a special milestone. It made $1 billion in sales, as Camuto had once **predicted**! Camuto died one year later at age 78. Simpson shared an Instagram post honoring him. "You are my **mentor**, my family, the creator of all my dreams," she said. "I will forever walk in your shoes. . . you made them." Months later, the Jessica Simpson Collection marked its ten-year anniversary.

FASHION FACT

From 2012 to 2013, Simpson starred as a judge on *Fashion Star*. Judges on this TV show reviewed clothing designed by contestants who hoped to convince department stores to sell their lines.

Simpson, husband Johnson, and children Maxwell and Ace attend a Jessica Simpson Collection event in 2013.

STEADY SUCCESS

Today, the Jessica Simpson Collection remains a steady success. In 2018, it featured items in 37 categories, including perfume and swimwear. In July of that year, Simpson **debuted** a cosmetics collection called Beauty Fiend. The line's first offerings were a variety of makeup brushes, including a set shaped like flowers.

No matter how much her brand expands, Simpson stays true to her American roots. In April 2018, she visited a department store in Nashville, Tennessee, to promote her spring clothing line. She invited personnel from a nearby military base to attend the event. Spouses of the personnel modeled in a pop-up fashion show at the store.

Simpson's family has also continued to grow. In March 2019, she and Johnson welcomed their third child, a daughter named Birdie.

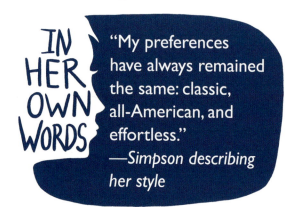

IN HER OWN WORDS

"My preferences have always remained the same: classic, all-American, and effortless."
—Simpson describing her style

In 2018, Simpson promoted her cosmetics collection Beauty Fiend at fashion and makeup festival Beautycon in California.

Simpson did not always dream of becoming a fashion icon. But her ability to connect to everyday women has made her one! Simpson's body-positive, down-to-earth fashion empire is a billion-dollar business that keeps growing.

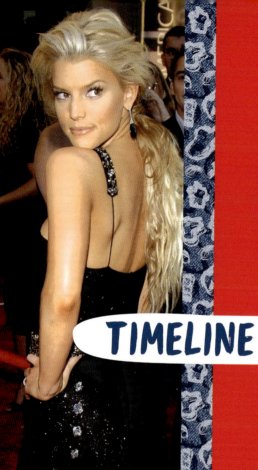

TIMELINE

1980 — Jessica Ann Simpson is born on July 10 in Abilene, Texas.

1992 — Jessica auditions for *The Mickey Mouse Club* but is not selected for the show.

1999 — Simpson releases her first album, *Sweet Kisses*. The song "I Wanna Love You Forever" is a hit.

2002 — Simpson marries singer Nick Lachey.

2003–2005 — Simpson and Lachey star on reality TV show *Newlyweds: Nick & Jessica*.

2005 — Simpson plays Daisy Duke in the film *The Dukes of Hazzard*.

- **2005** — Simpson releases failed lines JS by Jessica Simpson and Princy. Later in the year, she debuts the Jessica Simpson Collection shoe line.
- **2006** — The Jessica Simpson Collection expands to include clothing.
- **2010** — Simpson's TV documentary *The Price of Beauty* airs, exploring global beauty standards.
- **2012** — Simpson has a daughter, Maxwell, with Eric Johnson.
- **2013** — Simpson gives birth to son Ace.
- **2014** — The Jessica Simpson Collection makes $1 billion in sales.
- **2018** — Simpson launches a cosmetics line, Beauty Fiend.
- **2019** — Simpson has her third child, a daughter named Birdie.

GLOSSARY

accessible—being within reach.

audition—to give a trial performance showcasing personal talent as a musician, a singer, a dancer, or an actor. This performance is also called an audition.

bankrupt—legally declared unable to pay something owed.

CEO—chief executive officer. The person who makes the major decisions for running an organization or business.

debut—to present or perform something for the first time.

decade—a period of ten years.

ditzy—very silly or stupid.

documentary—a film or television series that artistically presents facts, often about an event or a person.

entrepreneur—one who organizes, manages, and accepts the risks of a business or an enterprise.

executive—someone who has one of the highest or most powerful jobs in a company or organization.

inclusive—welcoming to everyone.

market—to advertise or promote an item for sale. This process is called marketing.

mentor—a trusted adviser or guide.

negative—bad or hurtful.

potential—what a person is capable of achieving in the future.

predict—to declare in advance.

producer—a person who oversees or provides money for a play, television show, movie, or album.

ritual—a set form or order to a ceremony.

ONLINE RESOURCES

To learn more about Jessica Simpson, please visit **abdobooklinks.com** or scan this QR code. These links are routinely monitored and updated to provide the most current information available.

INDEX

advertising, 12, 14
albums
  In This Skin, 10
  Sweet Kisses, 10

body image, 4, 18, 20, 22, 27

Camuto, Vince, 14, 16, 17, 22, 24
Charming Shoppes, 14
Columbia Records, 8

Disney Channel, 6
Duke, Daisy, 11, 12, 16
Dukes of Hazzard, The, 11, 12

family, 6, 8, 10, 18, 22, 24, 26

fashion lines
  Beauty Fiend, 26
  Jessica Simpson Collection, 4, 16, 17, 18, 22, 24, 26
  JS by Jessica Simpson, 12
  Princy, 12

Johnson, Eric, 24, 26

Lachey, Nick, 10, 11
legal action, 14

Mickey Mouse Club, The, 6
Mottola, Tommy, 8

New York City, 22
Newlyweds: Nick & Jessica, 4, 10, 11, 16
98 Degrees, 10

personal style, 4, 12, 16, 18
Price of Beauty, The, 18, 19, 20

sales, 16, 24
singing career, 4, 6, 7, 8, 10
Soaries, DeForest "Buster," 7
social media, 24

Tarrant Apparel Group, 12, 14, 16
television career, 4, 10, 11, 16, 18, 19, 20
Tennessee, 26
Texas, 6, 22
Thailand, 19

VH1, 10